Record of the

Five First Saturdays

Devotion

Diana L. Ruzicka, RN
International Catholic Committee of Nurses
and Medico Social Assistants
(CICIAMS, INPO)

Diana L. Ruzicka Publisher
New Market, Alabama
Copies available at www.lulu.com/spotlight/Ruzicka

Illustration (page 3):
On June 13, 1929, at the Dorothean Convent Chapel
in Tuy, Spain, where Sister Lucia was a novice,
she was graced with a vision of the
Most Holy Trinity. Sister Lucia describes:

*Suddenly the whole chapel was illuminated by a
supernatural light, and above the altar appeared a
cross of light, reaching to the ceiling. In a brighter
light on the upper part of the cross, could be seen the
face of a man and his body as far as the waist, upon
his breast was a dove of light; nailed to the cross was
the body of another man. A little below the waist, I
could see a chalice and a large host suspended in the
air, onto which drops of blood were falling from the
face of Jesus Crucified and from the wound in His
side. These drops ran down onto the host and fell into
the chalice. Beneath the right arm of the cross was
Our Lady and in her hand was her Immaculate Heart.
(It was Our Lady of Fatima, with her Immaculate
Heart in her left hand, without sword or roses, but
with a crown of thorns and flames). Under the left arm
of the cross, large letters, as if of crystal clear water
which ran down upon the altar, formed these words:
'Grace and Mercy.' I understood that it was the
Mystery of the Most Holy Trinity which was shown to
me, and I received lights about this mystery which I
am not permitted to reveal."*

THE MOST HOLY TRINITY
Vision of Sister Lucia of Fatima Dorothean Convent - Tuy, Spain, 1929

And the Lord passed by Moses and He declared before Moses:
*"The Lord, the Lord, merciful and gracious, slow to anger,
abounding in steadfast love and faithfulness, keeping steadfast love
to a thousand generations and forgiving iniquities, transgressions and sins,
but by no means does He clear the guilty..."* Exodus 34:6-7

GOD LOVES YOU

CICIAMS General Secretariat
Palazzo San Calisto
00120 Vatican City
www.ciciams.org
ciciamsinternational12@gmail.com

Imprint: www.lulu.com/spotlight/Ruzicka
Compiled by Diana Ruzicka, MSN, MA, MA, RN
CICIAMS Secretary General, 2024

ISBN: 9780971007550

To the nurses of the International Catholic Committee
of Nurses and Medico Social Assistants (CICIAMS)
www.ciciams.org
may the Blessed Virgin Mary guide all nurses
to care for Jesus in the distressing disguise
of the poor and ill with compassion and charity.

In petition for the
Conversion of all people to Jesus Christ
and the
Triumph of the Immaculate Heart of Mary

Proceeds from the sale of this text are donated to
CICIAMS for the continued collaboration of
Catholic nurses across the world.

Quick Reference

First Saturday #1 - Date: _____

First Saturday #2 - Date: _____

First Saturday #3 - Date: _____

First Saturday #4 - Date: _____

First Saturday #5 - Date: _____

Preface

Conceived in 1928 and hosting our first world congress in Lourdes, France in 1933, CICIAMS is organized on the worldwide and international level as an association of national Catholic guilds of nurses, midwives and health workers. On August 27, 1935, His Holiness Pope Pius XI addressed 2000 nurses attending the second World Congress in Rome. His Holiness stressed the importance of nurses not only bringing health for the body but most importantly to bring life to the soul stating, *"And the treasure which your assistance must bring to the infirm is precisely that of spirituality, of the Christian supernatural, Christ."*

In his address two years later presented at the CICIAMS third World Congress in London, His Holiness Pope Pius XI specifically charged Catholic Nurses to guard against the eugenics and neo-malthusianism --- population control. He wrote to the assembly that it was *the duty of every Catholic nurse to belong to Catholic associations of nurses and to promote them in every way possible.*

Today nurses from four regions: Africa, Asia, Europe and Pan America represent the professional and Christian interests of its members. CICIAMS aims to promote members' spiritual welfare and ethical values; health and social measures of health in line with Catholic principles, and cooperation among member associations. At quadrennial World and Region Congresses member convene for professional development seminars. This publication is an effort to contribute to the spiritual development of our members. May God bless you.

Rosemary Khosi Mthethwa, MPH, PhD, RN
CICIAMS International President (2020-2028)
October 13, 2024, Kingdom of Eswatini

Introduction

In this new devotional booklet concerning Our Lady of Fatima's First Five Saturdays, Diana Ruzicka has created a new spiritual tool for us Catholics to remain faithful to the request of our Blessed Mother Mary. Over a hundred years have passed since our Blessed Mother originally made the request to observe the First Five Saturdays to the three children at Fatima on July 13, 1917 to promote world peace. Sadly, yet again in this first quarter of the 21st century our world is threatened to extinction by the war between Ukraine and Russia. Once more we need the loving help of our Blessed Mother to bring us children of Eve (Genesis 3:20) to her heart to find world peace, brotherly and sisterly love, and purity. Diana as a Catholic woman, mother, wife and nurse is promoting the mission of the Blessed Mother through Blessed Sr. Lucia in a new way to help us to grow spiritually at this time in human history through devotion to First Five Saturdays. Concerning the scriptural basis for devotions to the Blessed Mother I offer two passages; first, at the wedding feast at Cana, when Mary said to the servants, "Do whatever he says to do" (John 2:5); and secondly, on the Cross at Calvary when Jesus entrusted care of His mother Mary to us His disciples (John 19:27). I believe the dying wish of Jesus is asking us, his brothers and sisters (Luke 8:21) in the Catholic faith to listen and to love His mother as He had faithfully done in His own lifetime. We can fulfill this awesome responsibility to Jesus through the First Five Saturdays devotion. Diana's new devotional booklet is like a spiritual logbook with a checklist to keep track of our compliance. In Marian spirituality let us fulfill the dying wish of Jesus, the son of Mary, that we honor his mother.

---Fr. Ken Sleyman, MM
11Mar2023, Sapporo, Japan

This booklet provides space to record completion of the five consecutive first Saturday devotions as requested by the Blessed Virgin Mary in 1925. The history of this devotion is at the end of this booklet. A brief explanation of the devotion is below.

Summary of the Basic Requirements
On December 10, 1925, the Blessed Virgin Mary said to Sr. Lucia:
"Look, my daughter, at my Heart, surrounded with thorns with which ungrateful men pierce me at every moment by their blasphemies and ingratitude. You at least try to console me. Say that I promise to assist at the hour of death, with the graces necessary for salvation, all those who, on the 1st Saturday of five consecutive months:
1) shall confess [their sins],
2) receive Holy Communion,
3) recite five decades of the Rosary, and
4) keep me company for 15 minutes while meditating on the 15 mysteries of the Rosary, with the intention of making reparation to me."

On May 29-30, 1930, Jesus explained the reason for Five First Saturdays:
"Daughter, the motive is simple. There are five kinds of offenses and blasphemies spoken against the Immaculate Heart of Mary. Blasphemies:
(1) against her Immaculate Conception;
(2) against her perpetual virginity;
(3) against her divine maternity, refusing at the same time to accept her as the Mother of mankind;
(4) by those who try publicly to implant in the hearts of children an indifference, contempt, and even hate for this Immaculate Mother; and
(5) for those who insult her directly in her sacred images."

Five First Saturdays Devotion
Requirements Explained

Confession—eight (8) days before or after the First Saturday with the intention in your heart of making reparation and consoling Our Blessed Mother.

When Lucia asked Jesus if it might be valid to go to Confession within 8 days, He told her yes, and that it could be even longer still <u>as long as they are in the state of grace</u> when they receive Him [in the Eucharist] and **have the intention of making reparation to the Immaculate Heart of Mary**. So, if you cannot confess on the First Saturday itself, do so when you can. Heaven is looking for dispositions of mind and heart. Confess at least monthly.

Holy Communion — Receive Holy Communion on the First Saturday in a spirit of reparation—a spiritual communion will not suffice.

The Holy Rosary --- Pray five decades of the Holy Rosary with the intention of making reparation for offenses made against the Immaculate Heart of Mary.

Meditate 15 minutes — Keep Mary company by meditating for fifteen minutes on the mysteries of the Rosary. This meditation entails *thinking* or *reading meditatively* (frequently pausing to reflect on the material read), in order to dwell on one or more of the mysteries in Our Lady's life. The fifteen-minute meditation and the praying of the Holy Rosary are to be performed separately.

First Saturday #1

In reparation for the five kinds of offenses and blasphemies spoken against the Immaculate Heart of Mary:

(1) against her Immaculate Conception;
(2) against her perpetual virginity;
(3) against her divine maternity, refusing at the same time to accept her as the Mother of mankind;
(4) by those who try publicly to implant in the hearts of children an indifference, contempt, and even hate for this Immaculate Mother; and
(5) for those who insult her directly in her sacred images."

With the Intention of making reparation to the Blessed Virgin Mary complete the following:

    1) "confess [sins] (within 8 days)

All of the following on this Saturday:
    2) receive Holy Communion
    3) recite five decades of the Rosary, and
    4) keep me *[the Blessed Virgin Mary]* company for 15 minutes while meditating on the 15 mysteries of the Rosary, with the intention of making reparation to me."

    Date accomplished: _____
    (In pencil until all 5 consecutively accomplished)

Immaculate Conception

Bible:

And he came to her and said, "Hail, **full of grace**, the Lord is with you!" Luke 1:28.

(The Greek verb, kecharitōmenē, in English, "full of grace"; in Latin "plena gratia," is in the "perfect" tense which denotes a completed action the effects of which continue in the present. So Mary received grace in some complete way and remains completed in that grace. Mary was "completely, perfectly, enduringly endowed with grace).

The Holy Father Ex Cathedra Proclamation

"We declare, pronounce, and define that the doctrine which holds that the most Blessed Virgin Mary, in the first instance of her conception, by a singular grace and privilege granted by Almighty God, in view of the merits of Jesus Christ, the Savior of the human race, was preserved free from all stain of original sin, is a doctrine revealed by God and therefore to be believed firmly and constantly by all the faithful."

Pope Pius IX, *Ineffabilis Deus*, 8Dec1854/CCC 491

"Full of grace"" by this unusual form of greeting the archangel reveals Mary's special dignity and honour. The Fathers and Doctors of the Church "taught that this singular, solemn and unheard of greeting showed that all the divine graces reposed in the Mother of God and that she was adorned with all the gifts of the Holy Spirit," which meant that she "was never subject to the curse," that is, was preserved from all sin. These words of the archangel in this text constitute one of the sources which reveal the dogma of Mary's Immaculate Conception (cf. Pius IX, *Ineffabilis Deus*; Paul VI, *Creed of the People of God*).

Navarre Bible Commentary, Gospel & Acts, 345

First Saturday #2

In reparation for the five kinds of offenses and blasphemies spoken against the Immaculate Heart of Mary:

(1) against her Immaculate Conception;
(2) **against her perpetual virginity;**
(3) against her divine maternity, refusing at the same time to accept her as the Mother of mankind;
(4) by those who try publicly to implant in the hearts of children an indifference, contempt, and even hate for this Immaculate Mother; and
(5) for those who insult her directly in her sacred images."

With the Intention of making reparation to the Blessed Virgin Mary complete the following:

1) "confess [sins] (within 8 days)

All of the following on this Saturday:

2) receive Holy Communion
3) recite five decades of the Rosary, and
4) keep me *[the Blessed Virgin Mary]* company for 15 minutes while meditating on the 15 mysteries of the Rosary, with the intention of making reparation to me."

Date accomplished: _____
(In pencil until all 5 consecutively accomplished)

Perpetual Virginity

The NT often mentions Jesus' brethren (13:55; Mk 3:31; 6:3; Lk 8:19; Jn 2:12; 7:3; Acts 1:14; Gal 1:19). The Church maintains, however, that Jesus' Mother, Mary, remained a virgin throughout her life. These so-called brethren of Jesus are thus His relatives but not the children of Mary. Four observations support the Church's tradition:

1) These brethren are never called the children of Mary, although Jesus Himself is (Jn 2:1; 19:25; Acts 1:14).

2) Two names mentioned, James and Joseph, are sons of a different "Mary" in Mt 27:56 (Mk 15:40).

3) It is unlikely that Jesus would entrust His Mother to the Apostle John at His crucifixion if she had other natural sons to care for her (Jn 19:26-27).

4) The word brethren (Gk. Adelphoi) has a broader meaning than blood brother. Since ancient Hebrew had no word for "cousin" it was customary to use "brethren" in the Bible for relationships other than blood brothers. In the Greek OT, a "brother" can be a near related cousin (1 Chron 23:21-22), a more remote kinsman (Deu 23:7; 2 Kings 10:13-14), and uncle or nephew (Gen 13:8), or the relation between men bound by covenant (2 Sam 1:26; cf 1 Sam 18:3).

Continuing the OT tradition, the NT often uses "brother" or "brethren" in the wider sense. Paul uses it as a synonym for his Israelite kinsmen in Rm 9:3. It also denotes biologically unrelated Christians in the

New Covenant family of God (Rom 8:29; 12:1; Col 1:2; Heb 2:11; Jas 1:2; CCC 500).

There is no differentiation between cousin, nephew, brother in Hebrew and Aramaic. Thus, when the Bible mentions Jesus' brothers, these could be his cousins or other male relatives.

" 'You will conceive in your womb and bear a son, and you shall call his name, Jesus, ' she immediately asks: *'How can this be, since I have no husband?'* (Lk 1:31, 34). In the usual order of things motherhood is the result of mutual 'knowledge' between a man and a woman in the marriage union. Mary, firm in her resolve to preserve her virginity, puts this question to the divine messenger, and obtains from him the explanation: *'The Holy Spirit will come upon you'* — your motherhood will not be the consequent of matrimonial 'knowledge,' but will be the work of the Holy Spirit, the *'power of the Most High'* will *'overshadow'* the mystery of the Son's conception and birth; as the Son of the Most High, He is given to you exclusively by God, in a manner known to God. Mary, therefore, maintained her virginal *'I have no husband'* (cf. Lk 1:34) and at the same time became a Mother. Virginity and motherhood co-exist in her."

Mulieris Dignitatem (MD17)
(On the Dignity and Vocation of Women)

First Saturday #3

In reparation for the five kinds of offenses and blasphemies spoken against the Immaculate Heart of Mary:

(1) against her Immaculate Conception;

(2) against her perpetual virginity;

(3) **against her divine maternity, refusing at the same time to accept her as the Mother of mankind;**

(4) by those who try publicly to implant in the hearts of children an indifference, contempt, and even hate for this Immaculate Mother; and

(5) for those who insult her directly in her sacred images.

With the Intention of making reparation to the Blessed Virgin Mary complete the following:

1) "confess [sins] (within 8 days)

All of the following on this Saturday:

2) receive Holy Communion

3) recite five decades of the Rosary, and

4) keep me *[the Blessed Virgin Mary]* company for 15 minutes while meditating on the 15 mysteries of the Rosary, with the intention of making reparation to me."

Date accomplished: _____

(In pencil until all 5 consecutively accomplished)

Divine Maternity & Mother of Mankind

Divine Maternity

"Mary is truly the Mother of God."
>   Council of Ephesus, June 22, 431 A.D.
>   III Ecumenical Council

The Angel Gabriel to the Blessed Virgin Mary:
"And now, you will conceive in your womb and bear a son, and will call His name, 'Jesus.' He will be great, and will be called the Son of the Most High, and the Lord God will give to Him the throne of His ancestor David. He will reign over the house of Jacob forever, and His kingdom will never end." Mary said to the angel, "How can this be, since I am a virgin?" (Lk 1:31-34)
...The angel said to her, "The Holy Spirit will come upon you, and the power of the Most High will overshadow you; therefore, the child to be born will be holy; he will be called Son of God." (Luke 1:35)

Note: The conception of Jesus in the womb of the Blessed Virgin Mary was unique. No word(s) in the Bible are without significance. *"You will conceive in your womb."* Most children are conceived in the woman's fallopian tube where the male sperm and egg unite. Mary, however, conceived "in her womb" by "the power of the Most High." Her baby, the Christ child, the Savior of the world, by the grace of God, and power of the Holy Spirit was conceived in her uterus, in her womb, not in the fallopian tube, as is the case with the natural conception of human beings. Mary conceived the Son of God, the second person of the Blessed Trinity in her womb at the fullness of time. "Divine Maternity."

At the Third Ecumenical Council, the Church countered the Arian heresy championed by Nestorius, Bishop of Constantinople. The Church expressed the teaching of the apostles on the great mystery of the Incarnation, *"This is the true faith to believe and confess that our Lord, Jesus Christ, the Son of God, is God and man. Although at the same time God and man, there are not in Him two, but only one Christ. One absolutely, not by any confusion of substance, but by unity of person, that Jesus is God and man."* Jesus is one person with two natures, one human and one divine. A woman gives birth to a person (not to a "nature"). Mary is truly the Mother of God, Theotokos (God-bearer), as the III Ecumenical Council, proclaimed to the great joy of the people.

...the Word was made flesh, can mean nothing else but that He partook of flesh and blood like to us; He made our body His own, and came forth man from a woman, not casting off His existence as God, or His generation of God the Father, but even in taking to Himself flesh remaining what He was. This the declaration of the correct faith proclaims everywhere. This was the sentiment of the holy Fathers; therefore, they ventured to call the holy Virgin, the Mother of God, not as if the nature of the Word or His divinity had its beginning from the holy Virgin, but because of her was born that holy body with a rational soul, to which the Word being personally united is said to be born according to the flesh.

> The Epistle of St. Cyril to Nestorius
> https://conciliarpost.com/theology-
> spirituality/the-epistle-of-st-cyril-to-
> nestorius/

Mother of Mankind

When Jesus saw his mother and the disciple whom He loved standing beside her, He said to His mother, "Woman, here is your son." Then He said to the disciple, "Here is your mother." And from that hour the disciple took her into his own home (Jn 19:26-27).

The Blessed Virgin was left behind by Christ, in order to be the mother of the Apostles and the faithful, to gather the fallen, to comfort the afflicted, to support the stumbling, to advise the doubtful and the anxious, and to guide, instruct and inspire them in everything. Hence, she immediately gathered the Apostles who had dispersed when Christ was captured. She uplifted Peter, who was downcast on account of his denial of Christ, with the hope of forgiveness, and she assured all who were troubled by Christ's death through her faith in the resurrection of Christ which would soon come to pass. Then, when the leaders of the Jews imprisoned, scourged and killed the Apostles, she vividly experienced all these persecutions as though they were inflicted upon her, but she overcame them by her lofty spirit, and taught the Apostles by her word and example to overcome them.

Christ, foreseeing all these things said, "Woman," as if to say: O Mother, be henceforth that valiant and courageous woman, so that thou mayest be, in My place, the foundation, rock and pillar of My Church, that thou mayest support it with thy strength and mayest drive away and scatter all the storms of temptations that rage against her by thine assistance, counsel and prayers, not only now, but in all centuries to come, until the end of the world. That is why she is called in the Litanies and constantly invoked by the faithful and the entire Church as "Comforter of the afflicted. Refuge of sinners, Health of the sick, Tower of David, Ark of the Covenant, Help of Christians, Morning Star, Gate of Heaven, Mother most admirable, Virgin of virgins, Queen of Apostles, of Martyrs, of Confessors, and of All Saints."[2]

Mary is the mother of the fellow-Apostles, and of the other faithful, who are represented here in the person of John. Accordingly, all the faithful should fly to her with full confidence and love as St. Bernard teaches, whose words I have already cited. She is the true Eve of the faithful, *i.e.*, the mother of the living. Thus, all who are wise and the saints of every age have had recourse to her.[3]

A great sign appeared in the sky, a woman clothed with the sun, with the moon under her feet, and on her head a crown of twelve stars (Rev. 12:1).

The description of the woman indicates her heavenly glory, and the twelve stars of her victorious crown symbolize the people of God—the twelve patriarchs (cf. Gen 37:9) and the twelve apostles. And so, independently of the chronological aspects of the text, the Church sees in this heavenly woman the Blessed Virgin, "taken up body and soul into heavenly glory, when her earthly life was over, and exalted by the Lord as Queen over all things, that she might be the more fully conformed to her Son, the Lord of lords (cf. Rev. 19:16) and conqueror of sin and death" (*Lumen gentium*, 59). The Blessed Virgin is indeed the great sign, for as St. Bonaventure says, "God could have made none greater. He could have made a greater world and a greater heaven; but not a woman greater than his own mother" (*Speculum*, 8).[4]

First Saturday #4

In reparation for the five kinds of offenses and blasphemies spoken against the Immaculate Heart of Mary:

(1) against her Immaculate Conception;

(2) against her perpetual virginity;

(3) against her divine maternity, refusing at the same time to accept her as the Mother of mankind;

(4) **by those who try publicly to implant in the hearts of children an indifference, contempt, and even hate for this Immaculate Mother**; and

(5) for those who insult her directly in her sacred images."

With the Intention of making reparation to the Blessed Virgin Mary complete the following:

1) "confess [sins] (within 8 days)

All of the following on this Saturday:

2) receive Holy Communion

3) recite five decades of the Rosary, and

4) keep me *[the Blessed Virgin Mary]* company for 15 minutes while meditating on the 15 mysteries of the Rosary, with the intention of making reparation to me."

Date accomplished: _____

(In pencil until all 5 consecutively accomplished)

In Reparation for indifference, contempt & hate for the Immaculate Mother

Honor your father and mother. Mt. 15:4 & 19:19, Mk 7:10; Ephesians 6:2

"Who are my mother and my brothers?" he asked... "Whoever does God's will is my brother and sister and mother." (Mk 3:33, 35)

Some use the above verses to discount the high esteem in which Jesus honored His mother. However, who actually did the will of God most perfectly? The Blessed Virgin Mary. Who is the greatest woman in the Bible, of all time? It is not Esther, though Esther was indeed an exemplary woman who saved the Jewish people. The Blessed Virgin Mary is the greatest woman of all time. Four of the many reasons are listed below:
1) Her fiat (yes) brought forth the redemption of the whole human race. 2) She carried within her womb, as within a tabernacle of her body, God. 3) She is the new Eve, the mother of all the living. 4) By a singular grace of God, she was conceived free of the stain of sin. The following is an excerpt from *Ineffabilis Deus* promulgated by Pope Blessed Pius IX in 1854:

> "From the very beginning, and before time began, the eternal Father chose and prepared for his only-begotten Son a Mother in whom the Son of God would become incarnate and from whom, in the blessed fullness of time, he would be born into this world. Above all creatures did God so loved her that truly in her was the Father well pleased with singular delight. Therefore, far above all the angels

and all the saints so wondrously did God
endow her with the abundance of all
heavenly gifts poured from the treasury of his
divinity that this mother, ever absolutely free
of all stain of sin, all fair and perfect, would
possess that fullness of holy innocence and
sanctity than which, under God, one cannot
even imagine anything greater, and which,
outside of God, no mind can succeed in
comprehending fully."

Ineffabilis Deus
(The Immaculate Conception)
Pope Bl. Pius IX, 1854

First Saturday #5

In reparation for the five kinds of offenses and blasphemies spoken against the Immaculate Heart of Mary:

(1) against her Immaculate Conception;
(2) against her perpetual virginity;
(3) against her divine maternity, refusing at the same time to accept her as the Mother of mankind;
(4) by those who try publicly to implant in the hearts of children an indifference, contempt, and even hate for this Immaculate Mother; and
(5) **for those who insult her directly in her sacred images."**

With the Intention of making reparation to the Blessed Virgin Mary complete the following:

    1) "confess [sins] (within 8 days)

All of the following on this Saturday:
    2) receive Holy Communion
    3) recite five decades of the Rosary, and
    4) keep me *[the Blessed Virgin Mary]* company for 15 minutes while meditating on the 15 mysteries of the Rosary, with the intention of making reparation to me."

    Date accomplished: _____
    (In pencil until all 5 consecutively accomplished)

In Reparation for insults to her Sacred Images

St. Luke wrote the icon of the Blessed Virgin Mary and the infant Jesus commonly referred to as "the Black Madonna" or "Our Lady of Czestochowa." St. Helena is said to have brought it to Constantinople in the 4th century. It was owned by Charlemagne, then Prince Lev of Galicia (western Ukraine) where it was kept for almost six centuries in the royal palace at Belz. In 1382, it was moved to Czestochowa for safekeeping during a Tartar invasion. There it has remained. In 1430, the Hussite raiders slashed it and attempted to burn it. Thus the scar on the Blessed Virgin Mary's face. Many miracles are credited to The Black Madonna on behalf of those who prayed for her protection and intercession.

Do Catholic worship the portrait? No. That would be idolatry. Portraits, images and statues remind Christians of the individual in the picture they portray. Venerating images points to what they represent.

It was in the 8th century that the heresy of iconoclasm threatened the Church. The iconoclast heresy came originally from the Jews, Saracens (Muslims) and Manicheans. It infiltrated Christianity during the reign of Emperor Leo III (717-741).

Isaurian was a warlike prince who had a profound ignorance of religion and had the misguided belief that he would reform religion. When he became Emperor Leo III, he pronounced the Church custom of veneration of images as idolatrous and resolved to destroy images and statues of saints. In 726, he issued an edict that all images of Our Lord, of the Blessed Virgin, and of the saints be removed from the churches. When Pope St. Gregory II (715-731) attempted to educate the emperor, the emperor burnt all the sacred images in one of the public places of the city, and in the churches he whitewashed the walls, which were covered with precious paintings. He ordered that a large picture of our Lord, which had been erected in Constantinople at the entrance to the palace, be smashed.

On October 13, 787 A.D., three hundred and eighty-six bishops and procurators assembled in Nicaea in Bithynia (modern day Turkey) for the Seventh Ecumenical Council to address iconoclasm and, at the seventh session issued a definition of faith, concerning the veneration of holy images:

"We define with all certainty and diligence that as the figure of the precious and life-giving cross, so the veneration of holy images, both painted and of stone and of other proper material, should be set up in the holy churches of God, put on the sacred vessels and vestments, on the walls, and on tables, in houses and along the roads: that is, the image of our Lord God and Saviour Jesus Christ, and of our inviolate Lady, the holy Mother of God, and of the honorable angels, and of all holy and distinguished men. The more frequently they are seen by a pictorial representation, the more readily those who contemplate them, are excited to a remembrance of and desire for the prototypes, and to bestow upon them a respectful devotion; not, however, a "latria' (adoration), which is, according to our faith, and as is becoming bestowed upon the divine nature alone."(Oct 13, 787 A.D.)[5]

Types of veneration:
* Latria (adoration) - God alone
* Hyperdulia (special veneration) - Blessed Virgin Mary
* Dulia (veneration) - Angels and Saints

3) On each of the large beads, state the Mystery and pray **The Lord's Prayer** followed by **10-Hail Mary**'s on the small beads, then the **Glory Be** and the **Fatima Prayer** while meditating on each mystery with the intention of making reparation to the Blessed Virgin Mary.

4) After 5 decades end with the **Hail Holy Queen** & the "**O God....**"

2) On the large bead pray **The Lord's Prayer** followed by 3-**Hail Mary**'s on the small beads (for the theological virtues of Faith, Hope & Charity), then the **Glory Be.**

1) Make the **Sign of the Cross** & pray the **Apostles Creed**

The Most Holy Rosary

The Apostles Creed

I believe in God, the Father Almighty, Creator of heaven and earth; and in Jesus Christ, His only Son, our Lord: Who was conceived by the Holy Spirit, born of the Virgin Mary, suffered under Pontius Pilate, was crucified, died and was buried. He descended into hell, on the third day He rose again from the dead; He ascended into heaven, is seated at the right hand of God the Father Almighty; from thence He shall come to judge the living and the dead. I believe in the Holy Spirit, the Holy Catholic Church, the communion of Saints, the forgiveness of sins, the resurrection of the body, and life everlasting. Amen.

Source: "The Apostles' Creed is so called because it is rightly considered to be a faithful summary of the Apostles' faith. It is the ancient baptismal symbol of the Church of Rome. Its great authority arises from this fact: it is the Creed of the Roman Church, the See of Peter, the first of the apostles, to which he brought the common faith." (CCC194). St. Ambrose (337-397A.D.)

The Lord's Prayer (Mt. 6:9-13)

Our Father who art in heaven, hallowed be Thy name. Thy kingdom come. Thy will be done on earth, as it is in heaven. Give us this day our daily bread, and forgive us our trespasses, as we forgive those who trespass against us, and lead us not into temptation, but deliver us from evil. Amen.

Hail Mary (Lk 1:28 & Lk 1:42)
Hail Mary full of grace, the Lord is with thee. Blessed art thou among women and blessed is the fruit of thy womb, Jesus. Holy Mary, Mother of God, pray for us sinners now and at the hour of our death. Amen.

Glory Be to the Father and to the Son and to the Holy Spirit. As it was in the beginning, is now and ever shall be, world without end. Amen.

Fatima Prayer (July 13, 1917)
O My Jesus, forgive us our sins. Save us from the fires of hell. Lead all souls to Heaven, especially those in most need of Thy mercy.

The Blessed Virgin Mary under the title
"Our Lady of Fatima" July 13, 1917

Hail Holy Queen, Mother of Mercy, our life, our sweetness and our hope. To thee do we cry, poor banished children of Eve, to thee do we send up our sighs, mourning and weeping in this valley of tears. Turn then, most gracious advocate, thine eyes of mercy towards us, and after this our exile, show unto us the blessed fruit of thy womb, Jesus. O clement, O loving, O sweet Virgin Mary.
Pray for us O holy Mother of God
That we may be made worthy of the promises of Christ.
Let us Pray: O God, whose only begotten Son, by His life, death and resurrection, has purchased for us the rewards of eternal life; grant, we beseech Thee, that, meditating upon these mysteries of the Most Holy Rosary of the Blessed Virgin Mary, we may imitate what they contain and obtain what they promise, through the same Christ our Lord. Amen.

Mysteries of the Rosary

The Joyful Mysteries
(Monday & Saturday)

The Annunciation (Lk 1:28, 31-32)
 Fruit of the Mystery: Humility
The Visitation (Lk 1:42 & 45)
 Fruit: Love of Neighbor
The Nativity of Jesus (Lk 2:6-7)
 Fruit of the Mystery: Poverty
The Presentation (Lk 2:22-23)
 Fruit of the Mystery: Obedience
Finding of the Child Jesus in the Temple (Lk 2:46-47)
 Fruit: Joy in Finding Jesus

The Sorrowful Mysteries
(Tuesday & Friday)

The Agony in the Garden (Lk 22:44-45; Mt 26:36/39)
 Fruit of the Mystery: Sorrow for Sin
The Scourging at the Pillar (Jn 19:1)
 Fruit of the Mystery: Purity
Crowning with Thorns (Mt 27:28-29)
 Fruit of the Mystery: Courage
Carrying of the Cross (Jn 19:17-18)
 Fruit of the Mystery: Patience
The Crucifixion & Death (Lk 23:46)
 Fruit of the Mystery: Perseverance

The Glorious Mysteries
(Wednesday and Sunday)

The Resurrection of Our Lord (Mt 28:5-6; Mk 16:6)
    Fruit of the Mystery: Faith
The Ascension into Heaven (Mk 16:19; Lk 24:50-51)
    Fruit of the Mystery: Hope
Descent of the Holy Spirit (Acts 2:3-4)
    Fruit of the Mystery: Love of God
The Assumption of Mary (Judith 13:18 & 15:9-10)
    Fruit: Grace of a Happy Death
The Coronation of Mary (Rev 12:1)
    Fruit: Trust in Mary's Intercession

Mysteries of Light
(a.k.a. Luminous Mysteries)[6]
(Thursday)
(added by Pope St. John Paul II in 2002)

The Baptism of Jesus (Mat 3:16-17)
    Fruit: Openness to the Holy Spirit
Jesus Manifests his Divinity at the Wedding Feast at Cana (Jn 2:5-7)
    Fruit: To Jesus through Mary
Proclamation of the Kingdom (Mt. 10:7-8)
    Fruit: Repentance and Trust in God
The Transfiguration (Lk 9:29, 35)
    Fruit: Desire for Holiness
The Institution of the Eucharist (Lk 22:19-20)
    Fruit: Adoration

History of the Request for Five First Saturdays

On March 25, 2022, His Holiness Pope Francis consecrated Russia and the Ukraine to the Immaculate Heart of Mary in union with bishops, priests and laity across the world. The 2022 consecration was made at the request of the Ukrainian bishops. For over a month, Russia and the Ukraine were at war. Refugees, women and children, had flooded into the neighboring country of Poland. And the Poles graciously welcomed the refugees into their homes and shelters. Why was this request made by the Ukrainian bishops?

Between May 13, 1917 and October 13, 1917, the Blessed Virgin Mary appeared to three shepherd children: Lucia dos Santos (10), Francisco (9) and Jacinta (7) Marto, at the Cova da Iria near Fatima, Portugal. I chronicle these appearances and subsequent events in *"Our Lady of Fatima: 1917-2022."* The following is a synopsis of the appearance and words related to Jesus' desire to "establish in the world the devotion to Mary's Immaculate Heart.

On June 13, 1917, after reminding the children to pray the Rosary daily, the Blessed Virgin Mary mentioned that Jesus wanted to establish in the world a devotion to her Immaculate Heart. Lucia's memoirs record *"She opened her hands and pierced our hearts with the light that streamed from her palms. It seems then that the first purpose of this light was to give us a knowledge of a special love for the Immaculate Heart of Mary just as on two other occasions it gave us a knowledge of God and the mystery of the Holy Trinity. From that day on we felt in our hearts a deeper love for the Immaculate Heart of Mary. In front of the palm of Our Lady's right hand was a heart encircled by thorns which pierced it. We understood that this was the Immaculate Heart of Mary, outraged by the sins of humanity and seeking reparation."*

On July 13, 1917, she showed the children a vision of hell and stated, "You have seen hell where the souls of poor sinners go. To save them, **God wishes to establish in the world devotion to my Immaculate Heart**. If what I say to you is done, many souls will be saved and there will be peace. The war is going to end [World War I]; but if people do not cease offending God, a worse one will break out during the pontificate of Pius XI [World War II]. When you see a night illumined by an unknown light, know that this is the great sign given you by God that He is about to punish the world for its crimes by means of war, famine, and persecutions of the Church and of the Holy Father.

To prevent this, **I shall come to ask for the consecration of Russia to my Immaculate Heart and the Communion of Reparation on the First Saturdays**. If my requests are heeded, Russia will be converted and there will be peace; if not, she will spread her errors throughout the world, causing wars and persecutions of the Church. The good will be martyred, the Holy Father will have much to suffer, and various nations will be annihilated.

In the end, my Immaculate Heart will triumph. The Holy Father will consecrate Russia to me and she will be converted, and a period of peace will be granted to the world. In Portugal, the dogma of the Faith will always be preserved."

Eight years later on December 10, 1925, at the Dorothean Convent in Pontevedra, Spain, the Blessed Virgin Mary accompanied by the child Jesus appeared to Sister Lucia to request the Devotion to her Immaculate Heart. Sister Lucia wrote for her spiritual director, *"The most holy Virgin and by her side, elevated on a luminous cloud, was* [the Christ] *child. The most holy Virgin rested her hand on* [Sister Lucia's] *shoulder, and as she did so, she showed her heart encircled by thorns, which she was holding in her other hand. At the same time, the* [Christ] Child said: "Have compassion on the Heart of your most holy Mother, covered with thorns, with which ungrateful men pierce it at every moment, and there is no one to make an act of reparation to remove them."

Then the most holy Virgin said: "Look, my daughter, at my Heart, surrounded with thorns with which ungrateful men pierce me at every moment by their blasphemies and ingratitude. You at least try to console me and say that I promise to assist at the hour of death, with the graces necessary for salvation, all those who, on the 1st Saturday of five consecutive months, shall confess [their sins], receive Holy Communion, recite five decades of the Rosary, and keep me company for 15 minutes while meditating on the 15 mysteries of the Rosary, with the intention of making reparation to me."

When the promotion of this devotion had not moved forward two months later on February 15, 1926, the Christ Child appeared to Sister Lucia near the convent vegetable garden. She initially did not recognize Jesus until he asked, "And have you spread through the world what our heavenly Mother requested of you?"

She responded, "My Jesus, you know very well what my confessor said to me in the letter I read to You. He told me that it was necessary for this vision to be repeated, for further happenings to prove its credibility, and he added that Mother Superior, on her own, could do nothing to propagate this devotion."[7]

Jesus shared,

It is true, my daughter, that many souls begin the First Saturdays, but few finish them, and those who do complete them do so in order to receive the graces that are promised thereby. It would please Me more if they did five with fervor and wish the intention of making reparation to the Heart of your heavenly Mother, than if they did fifteen in a tepid and indifferent manner.

It is true your Superior alone can do nothing, but with My grace she can do all. It is enough that your confessor gives you permission and that your Superior speak of it, for it to be believed, even without people knowing to whom it has been revealed.[7]

Three and a half years later on June 13, 1929, while Sister Lucia, at this time a novice with the Dorothean Sisters, was praying in the convent chapel in Tuy, Spain she was given a vision of the Trinity. (See cover and cover description).

After the vision of the Trinity, our Lady told Sister Lucia to ask the Holy Father to make the consecration of Russia: "The moment has come in which God asks the Holy Father, in union with all the bishops of the world, to <u>make the consecration of Russia to my Immaculate Heart</u>, promising to save it by this means. There are so many souls whom the Justice of God condemns for sins committed against me, that I have come to ask reparation: sacrifice yourself for this intention and pray."

The next year on May 29-30, 1930, in Tuy, Spain, Sister Lucia received interior knowledge regarding her confessor Fr. Jose Bernardo Goncalves' query as to why FIVE Saturdays and not 7 or 9 were requested in honor of the sorrow of Our Lady. Sister Lucia described a mystical experience she had when praying to our Lord in the Most Blessed Sacrament,

> *"Remaining in the chapel with our Lord, part of the night of the 29th-30th of the month of May, 1930, talking to our Lord about* [some of those] *questions, I suddenly felt possessed more intimately by the Divine Presence; and if I am not mistaken, the following was revealed to me"*: **"Daughter, the motive is simple. There are five kinds of offenses and blasphemies spoken against the Immaculate Heart of Mary: blasphemies**
> **(1) against her Immaculate Conception;**
> **(2) against her perpetual virginity;**
> **(3) against her divine maternity, refusing at the same time to accept her as the Mother of mankind;**
> **(4) by those who try publicly to implant in the hearts of children an indifference, contempt, and even hate for this Immaculate Mother; and**
> **(5) for those who insult her directly in her sacred images."**[8]

Our Lord ended this communication by telling Sister Lucia that it was His own mother who asked for these acts of reparation in order to move him to "forgive those souls who have the misfortune of offending her." Those who commit such blasphemies against our Lady are in grave jeopardy of losing their souls, for these sins seriously offend God Himself. In spite of these terrible indignities, it is our Lady, as the Blessed Mother, even of those who offend her so grievously, who is concerned for their eternal salvation.[8]

Ten years later on Mary 18, 1939, Sister Lucia described in a letter to Fr. Goncalves why Jesus would not convert Russia without the Holy Father making the consecration, "Because I want My whole Church to acknowledge that consecration as a triumph of the Immaculate Heart of Mary, so that it may extend its cult later on, and put the devotion of this Immaculate Heart beside the devotion to My Sacred Heart." Sr. Lucia pleaded, *"But my God, the Holy Father probably won't believe me, unless You Yourself, move him with a special inspiration."* Jesus responded, The Holy Father, pray very much for the Holy Father. He will do it, but it will be too late. Nevertheless, the Immaculate Heart of Mary will save Russia. It has been entrusted to her.

First Saturday Devotion

And thus in 1926 began the promotion of the consecutive Five First Saturday devotion; and the request for the consecration of Russia to Mary's Immaculate Heart followed in 1929. In regards to the devotion, honoring the Immaculate Heart of Mary was not new.

St. Mechtilde (1241-1298), St. Gertrude the Great (1256-1302), and St. Bridget of Sweden (1303-1373) fostered this devotion in their writings and private revelations. St Bernadine of Siena (1380-1444) was given the title, "Doctor of the Immaculate Heart of Mary," due to his love for and writing and preaching on the Blessed Virgin Mary's Heart. St. Francis de Sales (1567-1622) designed the crest of the Visitation Order that he founded with the two hearts of Jesus and Mary united together. St. John Eudes (1601-1680) was influenced by St. Francis de Sales and received the title, "Apostle of the Immaculate Heart," due to his work in establishing the liturgical devotion to the Immaculate Heart of Mary. Through his efforts in the 1600's, devotion to the Immaculate Heart was added to the Holy Sacrifice of the Mass and the Divine Office (Liturgy of the Hours). Official Saturday devotion to Our Lady traces its origin at least to 1892 when Pope Leo XIII granted the faithful a plenary indulgence for 15 consecutive Saturdays in honor of Our Lady of the Rosary. Pope Pius X granted a plenary indulgence for 12 First Saturdays in honor of Our Lady. And in 1905, Pope St. Pius X did the same. On June 13, 1912, Pope St. Pius X changed the indulgence from one of honor to a devotion of reparation to Our Lady. Pope Benedict XV added a plenary indulgence at the hour of death with specific requirements. Then it was on June 13, 1917, the Blessed Virgin Mary, herself formally requested the FIVE CONSECUTIVE first Saturdays.[1]

Consecration of Russia

Regarding the consecration of Russia to the Immaculate Heart of Mary. The consecration was attempted by Pope Pius XII (1942) and Pope Paul VI (1967), but neither followed the full instructions of the Blessed Virgin Mary which required that "Russia" be consecrated to the Immaculate Heart of Mary in union with the bishops. Pope St. John Paul II performed three consecrations following the May 13, 1981, assassination attempt on his life: on June 7, 1981, the Solemnity of Pentecost; on May 13, 1982, in Fatima and on March 15, 1984. It was reported that in 1989, Sister Lucia affirmed the final consecration. There continued, however, to be divergent opinions whether the consecration was accomplished since Russia was not specifically mentioned by name. Clearly, by the 1980's, Russia had spread her communist atheist errors throughout the world and even in the Church.

At the request of the bishops of the Ukraine, on March 25, 2022, Feast of the Annunciation, His Holiness Pope Francis performed the consecration of Russia to the Immaculate Heart of Mary in union with bishops around the world who chose to participate. He clearly mentioned Russia and the Ukraine in this beautiful prayer which included the following phrase:

> *Therefore, Mother of God and our Mother, to your Immaculate Heart we solemnly entrust and consecrate ourselves, the Church and all humanity, especially Russia and Ukraine. Accept this act that we carry out with confidence and love. Grant that war may end and peace spread throughout the world.*[9]

Now each person has their personal responsibility to complete the Five consecutive First Saturday Devotions. Jesus had stated that people begin and do not complete the five consecutive Saturday devotions.

This booklet is an effort to facilitate the completion of the Five First Saturdays. Write the dates in pencil until you complete five consecutively. Events will occur that interrupt the five consecutive Saturdays but don't let this discourage you. Begin again. Spouses, children and relatives should commit to complete this devotion together.

Diana L. Ruzicka, RN
CICIAMS Secretary General

Meditation by His Holiness Pope Benedict XVI
Mary, Star of Hope; Spe Salve 49

49. With a hymn composed in the eighth or ninth century, thus for over a thousand years, the Church has greeted Mary, the Mother of God, as "Star of the Sea": *Ave Maris Stella*. Human life is a journey. Towards what destination? How do we find the way? Life is like a voyage on the sea of history, often dark and stormy, a voyage in which we watch for the stars that indicate the route. The true stars of our life are the people who have lived good lives. They are lights of hope. Certainly, Jesus Christ is the true light, the sun that has risen above all the shadows of history. But to reach him we also need lights close by—people who shine with his light and so guide us along our way. Who more than Mary could be a star of hope for us? With her "yes" she opened the door of our world to God himself; she became the living Ark of the Covenant, in whom God took flesh, became one of us, and pitched his tent among us (cf. *Jn* 1:14).

50. So we cry to her: Holy Mary, you belonged to the humble and great souls of Israel who, like Simeon, were "looking for the consolation of Israel" (*Lk* 2:25) and hoping, like Anna, "for the redemption of Jerusalem" (*Lk* 2:38). Your life was thoroughly imbued with the sacred scriptures of Israel which spoke of hope, of the promise made to Abraham and his descendants (cf. *Lk* 1:55). In this way we can appreciate the holy fear that overcame you when the angel of the Lord appeared to you and told you that you would give birth to the One who was the hope of Israel, the One awaited by the world. Through you, through your "yes", the hope of the ages became

reality, entering this world and its history. You bowed low before the greatness of this task and gave your consent: "Behold, I am the handmaid of the Lord; let it be to me according to your word" (*Lk* 1:38). When you hastened with holy joy across the mountains of Judea to see your cousin Elizabeth, you became the image of the Church to come, which carries the hope of the world in her womb across the mountains of history. But alongside the joy which, with your *Magnificat,* you proclaimed in word and song for all the centuries to hear, you also knew the dark sayings of the prophets about the suffering of the servant of God in this world. Shining over his birth in the stable at Bethlehem, there were angels in splendour who brought the good news to the shepherds, but at the same time the lowliness of God in this world was all too palpable. The old man Simeon spoke to you of the sword which would pierce your soul (cf. *Lk* 2:35), of the sign of contradiction that your Son would be in this world. Then, when Jesus began his public ministry, you had to step aside, so that a new family could grow, the family which it was his mission to establish and which would be made up of those who heard his word and kept it (cf. *Lk* 11:27f). Notwithstanding the great joy that marked the beginning of Jesus's ministry, in the synagogue of Nazareth you must already have experienced the truth of the saying about the "sign of contradiction" (cf. *Lk* 4:28ff). In this way you saw the growing power of hostility and rejection which built up around Jesus until the hour of the Cross, when you had to look upon the Saviour of the world, the heir of David, the Son of God dying like a failure, exposed to mockery, between criminals. Then you received the word of Jesus:

"Woman, behold, your Son!" (*Jn* 19:26). From the Cross you received a new mission. From the Cross you became a mother in a new way: the mother of all those who believe in your Son Jesus and wish to follow him. The sword of sorrow pierced your heart. Did hope die? Did the world remain definitively without light, and life without purpose? At that moment, deep down, you probably listened again to the word spoken by the angel in answer to your fear at the time of the Annunciation: "Do not be afraid, Mary!" (*Lk* 1:30). How many times had the Lord, your Son, said the same thing to his disciples: do not be afraid! In your heart, you heard this word again during the night of Golgotha. Before the hour of his betrayal he had said to his disciples: "Be of good cheer, I have overcome the world" (*Jn* 16:33). "Let not your hearts be troubled, neither let them be afraid" (*Jn* 14:27). "Do not be afraid, Mary!" In that hour at Nazareth the angel had also said to you: "Of his kingdom there will be no end" (*Lk* 1:33). Could it have ended before it began? No, at the foot of the Cross, on the strength of Jesus's own word, you became the mother of believers. In this faith, which even in the darkness of Holy Saturday bore the certitude of hope, you made your way towards Easter morning. The joy of the Resurrection touched your heart and united you in a new way to the disciples, destined to become the family of Jesus through faith. In this way you were in the midst of the community of believers, who in the days following the Ascension prayed with one voice for the gift of the Holy Spirit (cf. *Acts* 1:14) and then received that gift on the day of Pentecost. The "Kingdom" of Jesus was not as might have been imagined. It began in that hour, and of this "Kingdom" there will be no end. Thus you remain in the midst of the disciples as their Mother, as the Mother of hope. Holy Mary, Mother of God, our Mother, teach us to believe, to hope, to love with you. Show us the way to his Kingdom! Star of the Sea, shine upon us and guide us on our way!

References:

1) Catherine Moran. The Rich History of Devotion to the Immaculate Heart. World Apostolate of Fatima, U.S.A. Accessed 7 July 2022. https://www.bluearmy.com/the-rich-history-of-devotion-to-the-immaculate-heart/

2) Michael J. Miller (2008). *The Great Commentary of Cornelius a Lapide: The Holy Gospel According to Saint John.* Fitzwilliam, New Hampshire: Loreto Publications, 734

3) Ibid, 736

4) Navarre Bible Commentary, *The Revelation to John (The Apocalypse)*, New York: Scepter Publishers, 81.

5) Father Clement Raab, O.F.M. (2012). *The Twenty Ecumenical Councils*. Fitzwilliam, New Hampshire, Loreto Publications, 32.

6) Pope St. John Paul II (2002). *Rosarium Virginis Mariae* (On the Most Holy Rosary). Accessed 7 July 2022. https://www.vatican.va/content/john-paul-ii/en/apost_letters/2002/documents/hf_jp-ii_apl_20021016_rosarium-virginis-mariae.html

7) Santos, Lucia dos (2006). *Fatima in Lucia's Own Words: Lucia's Memoirs, Volume II*. 4th ed. Edited by Fr. Louis Kondor, SVD. Translated by Dominican Nuns of Perpetual Rosary and Dominican Nuns of Mosteiro de Santa Maria. Fatima: Secretariado dos Pastorinhos, 196.

8) Apostoli, .C.F.R., Fr. Andrew (2010). *Fatima for Today: The Urgent Marian Message of Hope.* San Francisco, Ignatius Press, 157.

9) Pope Francis. (25 March 2022). *Act of Consecration to the Immaculate Heart of Mary.* Accessed 3 July 2023. https://www.vatican.va/content/francesco/en/prayers/documents/20220325-atto-consacrazione-cuoredimaria.html.

10) Pope Benedict XVI (30 November 2007). *In Hope We Were Saved. Spe Salve.* Accessed 13Oct2024. https://www.vatican.va/content/benedict-xvi/en/encyclicals/documents/hf_ben-xvi_enc_20071130_spe-salvi.html